D1512536

PRAYERS TO
THE NATURE SPIRITS

PRAYERS TO THE NATURE SPIRITS

Julia Cameron

RENAISSANCE BOOKS
Los Angeles

Library of Congress Cataloging-in-Publication Data
Cameron, Julia.
    Prayers to the nature spirits / Julia Cameron.
        p.   cm.
    ISBN 1-58063-047-2 (alk. paper)
    1. Nature—Prayer-books and devotions—English.
    2. Children—Prayer-books and devotions—English. I. Title.
BL435. C35   1999
291.4'33—dc21   98-51022
                                                  CIP
                                                  AC

10 9 8 7 6 5 4 3 2 1
Design by Lisa-Theresa Lenthall

Distributed by St. Martin's Press
Manufactured in the United States of America
First Edition

I dedicate this book to Timothy Wheater
Who asked me to write some prayers in meter.

CONTENTS

A   WORD   TO   READERS

Since the beginning of time, the natural world has been our teacher. Parents have used the creatures of nature to instruct their children in the lessons of life. Now that many of us and our children live in urban environments, we no longer have free access to our teachers in the natural world. For this reason, I have written this book, hoping with the tools of rhyme, humor, and careful observation, to allow the nature teachers to teach through my work in a playful yet memorable way.

The prayers are set in rhyme because rhyme is what the child's mind most easily remembers. (For many of us, the only well-remembered childhood prayer is the rhymed prayer, *Now I lay me down to sleep / I pray the Lord my soul to keep. . . .*)

While the prayers are intended to be read aloud to children, they are titled and organized according to theme, not animal. In this way, the book is able to function on two levels: as a teacher to young children and as an adult companion to the parent who reads aloud.

PRAYERS TO
THE NATURE SPIRITS

PRAYER FOR TENACITY

This is a prayer to the God of Ant

Who doesn't know the words "I can't."

This is a prayer for stubbornness

That always answers "no" with "yes."

Ants build cities out of sand.

Ants sing ditties with "I can."

Ants never think about the odds.

Ants know we're mortal but think they're gods.

Ants teach us patience, ants teach us strive.

Ants teach the power of being alive.

God of Ant, please teach me now,

The power of "yes" instead of "how?"

Where there's a will, there is a way.

That's the prayer ants always say.

continued

"I can, I will, I will, I can—"

That builds castles out of sand.

"I will, I can, I can, I will—"

God of Ant, teach me this skill.

Ant's a steady optimist.

He simply knows he is the best.

God of Ant, teach me to know

I'm much more than I ever show.

PRAYER FOR ACUITY

This is a prayer to the God of Bat,
The one who thrives in basic black.
This is a prayer to who flies by night,
The one who sees with sightless sight.
Grant me, Bat, your keen antenna
To help me see the shape I'm in.
A sense of sonar would be great
To help me pick the course to take.
Brother Bat, you caped crusader.
Let me learn your gift for radar.
Teach me, Bat, to check the sound
Of all the things that I'm around.
Give me, Bat, your sound advice
I know you're more than flying mice!

PRAYER FOR SELF-INITIATIVE

This is a prayer to the God of Cat,

The one who knows precisely that

Freedom's where the best game lies,

And this is why it's no surprise,

Cats contain more opinions

Than the layers of many onions.

"I'll decide," is what Cats say.

You bid them, "Come," they go away.

Dog's obedient, Cat's a prowler.

Though they may wear someone's collar,

Cats remember who knows best—

And it's Cat as you have guessed!

Cats keep counsel with themselves.

Cat's more prankish than the elves.

I'd ask you, Cat, to mentor me

But only at your liberty.

God of Cat, I'll bring you nip,

If you just let some guidance slip.

God of Cat, you and your ilk

Lap up wisdom just like milk.

You with nine lives know the best

What to share with all the rest.

God of Cat, I'll fetch a saucer,

If you'll only make me wiser.

I won't beg and I won't plead.

Respect is what a good Cat needs.

So if you could just share a whisker,

I'll be purrfect, you just whisper.

PRAYER FOR COOPERATION

This is a prayer to the Dolphin God,

The one who has a glistening nod.

Dolphins are sleek and they speak in a squeak.

Dolphins like sharing the secrets they keep.

(They've been talking to humans since we

were all Greek!)

Dolphins have brains far larger than man

And they try to teach humans whenever

they can.

They think using pictures they send like TV.

What they call talking is telepathy.

Dolphins are peaceful, generous friends.

They've rescued poor swimmers

from having sad ends.

Dolphins hold wisdom they share with
the stars.

They go there on light beams the way we
use cars.

Dolphins are messengers bringing the news

We all can evolve if we only so choose.

Dolphins are playful. Their own hearts
are light.

(Even people feel better when they do
what's right.)

Dolphins are teachers. Their students are we.

They say, "Learn to play nicely and then
you'll be free."

PRAYER FOR PROTECTION

This is a prayer to the God of Bear

The wooly brute who roars, "I dare!"

Bear's double-natured as all of us know—

Protective but fierce to outsiders and so,

Lord of All Bruins, please gift me with
  knowledge

Of when I should leave you alone with that
  porridge.

Bears make good parents; they baby their cubs.

Dads take them fishing; Moms dig for grubs.

And, should a sudden sweet tooth crop up,

Bears will raid beehives for honey enough—

Bears will scare campers and hikers beware!

Nothing is scarier than a grizzly, so there!

Caution's the keyword when dealing
with Bears.
Bears are confusing: a monster who cares.
God of the Bear, help me dare like you do
To be cheerful, hardworking, and still
playful too.
Teach me like you to protect what I love—
And teach me to savor the sight of a grub.
Lordly yet lowly, what a mixture you carry—
A lovable teddy who's also quite scary.
Fur, fang, and claw, you sure fill me with awe.
God of Bear, spare me the swipe of your paw.
Teach me, Oh Bear, to love with discretion—
And call on your powers when I need
protection.

PRAYER TO BE OF SPIRITUAL SERVICE

God of Horse, God of Steed,

Teach me by your strength and deed.

Willing Partner, Loving Mate,

Teach me to cooperate.

Show me by your dignity,

I can serve and still be free.

Swift as wind and soft as hay,

You teach me "yes" by saying "neigh."

Noble creature filled with power,

Teach me, too, to gently flower.

Satin-coated, silken-maned,

Wild at heart though gently tamed,

Teach me by your steady stride

To choose integrity not pride.

Lastly, teach me by your hooves,

We become just what we choose.

PRAYER FOR DARING

This is a prayer to the God of Flea

Who doesn't know, "Oh, Pardon Me."

Flea gets attention; there's no doubt of that.

Flea makes you tickle; Flea makes you scratch.

Flea can move mountains or even that dog—

A moment ago it slept like a log.

Then Flea gave the signal; Flea gave a bite.

The Dog started howling at all that's in sight.

God of the Flea, pay attention to me!

Teach me to always ignore all the odds—

Like the size of a Flea and the size of a Dog.

God of the Flea, teach me just how to nudge

So that I can move mountains others

   can't budge.

Teach me, Oh Flea, to be true to my goal.

Scratch the itch that's the twitch at the root
of my soul.

PRAYER FOR LOYAL COMMITMENT

This is a prayer to the God of Dogs,

The one who knows we're all cogs

In a larger wheel that's called creation,

A wheel that's served by our devotion.

Teach me, Dog, with sympathy,

A way to learn your empathy.

Teach me patience, teach me wait.

Teach me love what's on my plate.

Teach me bark and teach me howl.

Teach me grumble, teach me growl.

Teach me, Dog, communicate!

Indicate what's bad, what's great.

Teach me, Dog, to gently wag

Friends' spirits, as you do, when they sag.

Teach me yelp and teach me help.

Teach me, Dog, to be myself—

Dogged in my loyalty,

Devoted friend and family.

PRAYER TO SEIZE THE MOMENT

This is a prayer to the God of Rat,

While some go hungry, you grow fat.

Sleek and sneaky like an eel,

Your shadow coat can help conceal

The cunning way you find the paths

Through the garbage near the trash.

What we discard, you find with glee.

Our reject is your delicacy.

God of Rat with awesome teeth,

There is nothing that's beneath

Your beady gaze, your greedy paws—

A moment, Rat, for our applause!

In many ways you're quite discreet

And leave us with a cleaner street.

Ruthless Rat, you make your way.

Your message is, "Who, me, obey?"

If there's a lesson I could learn,

It's see the good in every turn.

Much of what we throw away

Could serve us still another day.

Teach me, Rat, to seize the day

And not to throw the best away.

Wiley Rat, you are quite prudent.

That's why you're a well-fed rodent.

PRAYER FOR INTEGRITY

This is a prayer for Lion and Tiger.

I've got a lot to learn from either.

Lion, teach me in my pride,

To care for others at my side.

Tiger, teach me by your stripes,

To draw the line between wrong and right.

Great Cats, teach me by your claws

To stop before anger and take a pause.

By your giant roar instruct,

How to tell folks, "That's enough!"

Teach me by your solitude

To just withdraw and not be rude.

Jungle's King and India's Queen,

Help me say just what I mean.

By your natures you are known.

Your lesson is, "to each its own."

PRAYER FOR PATIENCE

This is a prayer to the God of Elephant,

Of all God's creatures the most relevant

To teaching lessons regarding patience

Since Elephants live to be very ancient.

With legs like tree trunks and a hose

    for a nose,

Elephant's stared at wherever he goes.

A grey Goliath, a moving mountain,

Elephant teaches us all by counting

Very carefully the steps he takes.

An Elephant can't afford mistakes.

With tusks like sabers of gleaming ivory,

The Elephant trumpets his will most mightily,

But like the Whale, his sea-borne brother,

Elephant's most at home a lover.

Pachyderm's his other title

And Elephant's lesson is quite vital:

Live each day an open channel

Then you'll be a long-lived mammal.

PRAYER FOR PLUCK

This is a prayer to the God of Mouse,

The one who likes to share our house.

Mouse is tiny, but Mouse is bold.

He doesn't care how much we scold.

Mouse lays claim to kitchen stoves.

If you've got one Mouse, you've got droves.

Mouse creeps round corners, hides in pots.

Cupboards are a hiding spot.

Mouse dines on crumbs of what we ate.

Mouse loves when you don't clean your plate.

Only Cat can scare a Mouse.

The rest of us can only grouse.

"Pesky Mouse, please go away!

Don't make me use a trap today!"

PRAYER FOR QUICK WITS

This is a prayer to the God of Frog,

The one who lives in a slimey bog.

Frogs are slippery. Frogs are quick.

Frogs like to jump or else they sit

Watching with their bulging eyes.

You cannot take Frog by surprise.

Frog's a singer since first he spoke.

He cleared his throat and made a croak.

Frogs in chorus pass summer nights.

Frogs don't bore us with their delight

In catching flies and chasing bugs.

Frog's an expert at all he does.

Frog's high and mighty when he leaps.

I only wonder when he sleeps!

PRAYER FOR GENEROSITY

This is a prayer to the God of Cow
Whose message is "I allow."
With patient gaze and simple calm,
Your presence is a gentle balm.
In grassy fields your cud you chew.
Teach me, Cow, to think things through.
Pouring forth your silken milk,
You never cry over what's been spilt.
Your steady flow, a constant blessing,
Pours forth to all, no second guessing.
Cow, you serve through constancy.
I'd like to learn the same for me.
Grant me, Cow, your mellow mood
So I can practice brotherhood.

PRAYER FOR CAUTION

This is a prayer to the God of Owl,

The bird who has such a secretive scowl.

Owl is mysterious. Owl flies by night.

Owl hunts for mice by the palest moonlight.

Owl has soft feathers but terrible claws.

Owl teaches us there is meaning in laws,

Meaning be careful and on the alert.

Owl teaches caution so we won't be hurt.

Owl is a warning. Owl is a guide.

Owl says good judgment must be applied.

Owl rules the twilight, the time in between.

Owl teaches prudence of when to be seen.

Owl is a hunter. Beware to Owl's prey.

Owl says be careful of just where you play.

continued

Owls can be scary. Their gaze is a dare.

Owl says be wary and care when you dare!

PRAYER FOR HEALTHY BOUNDARIES

God of Needle, God of Tine,

God of Prickly Porcupine,

Prickly Pillow, Warning Bush,

Teach me how to say, "Too much."

Peaceful creature sleek by choice,

Like you, let me, a warning voice.

Rattle saber, rustle quill!

Say, "If you don't, you know I will."

God of Needle, God of Tine,

Good boundaries are a friend of mine.

Teach me temperance!

Teach me space!

Teach me, please, to claim my place.

PRAYER FOR THE LONGER VIEW

God of Giraffe, nature's portable tree,
Since you can see things more clearly
    than me,
Please use your height to give me perspective.
God of Giraffe, make your vision protective!
What's plain to you as you peer from the sky,
Is harder to view well for us smaller fry.

You can see distance and even horizon.
Life down below can be much more
    surprising.
God of Giraffe, your view is refreshing.
This I can tell just from how you are dressing.
God of Giraffe, does your coat of bold plaid
Strike you as being especially mad?

Or did your spots like all plots disappear

When viewed from an altitude higher

   than here?

Mad plaid on pipe stems could be quite a gaffe

But you, the Giraffe, always get the last laugh.

"I saw it coming," you say of trends.

We'll all dress like you do before it all ends!

God of Giraffe, the last laugh and the

   grandeur,

Please give me a goose or else give me a

   gander.

God of Giraffe, help me to spot the joke

And laugh like you do at us short-sighted folk.

God of Giraffe, let me share your

   clairvoyance—

Or barring that, give the gift of avoidance!

Master of Tall, share your map of the future!

Gift me with insight, you farseeing creature!

PRAYER FOR
HIGHER VISION

God of Falcon, Hawk, and Eagle,

Help me learn from you what's regal.

Lofty, soaring, flying high,

Help me see things with your eye.

Give me grace to see the distance

I must travel in each instance.

Guide me when to float away,

When to strike like bird of prey.

From you let me learn the vision

To act and react with precision.

God of Falcon, Hawk, and Eagle,

Talons sharp as any needle,

Grant to me your surgeon's skill

At discerning which things will

Work their way to right direction

Without my timely intersection.

Teach me, God of Air and Sky,

When to dally, when pass by.

Teach me, finally, Windborne Lords,

To have the faith of soaring birds—

Trusting to invisible winds,

Higher Forces, Higher Friends.

Give me grace to fly with you

And gain perspective as I do.

PRAYER FOR DISCERNMENT

This is a prayer to the God of Fishes

Some seem friends, some seem vicious.

Some like Angels float quite near.

Others bite and cause me fear.

A Barracuda in a mood,

A Shark that's seen its breakfast food,

A Moray Eel, a Manta Ray—

These fishes tell me, "Stay away!"

The Pilot Fish, the Zippy Zebra—

They seem to say, "So glad to meet ya!"

God of Fishes, based on this,

Help me know which fish to miss!

PRAYER FOR BALANCE

🌰

God of Sea Lion, God of Seal,

Velvet-coated, plush but real,

Sleek as any living thing,

You spend your days remembering

To warn all sailors off the rocks,

To spare their ships from shipwreck's cost.

Lion-throated, bellowed loud,

You strictly, sternly, do the job.

Then with sudden ocean spray,

You dip below and start to play,

Balanced on your back in waves,

You fan yourself like sultan's slaves.

Then when one of you feels hunger,

You dive below and fish down under.

continued

Abalone from the shell?

An appetizer you love well.

God of Sea Lion, God of Seal,

Help me find my balance wheel!

Teach me work and play by turns.

That's the lesson your tribe learns.

PRAYER FOR
BOLDNESS

This is a prayer to the God of Pig

Whose motto is, "Dare to be Big!"

Let others be modest! Let others be shy!

Pigs live to teach us it's better to try.

Pigs wiggle through fences!

Pigs climb into troughs!

Pigs like to turn feeding pens into small bogs.

Pigs like to get filthy!

Pigs wallow in mud!

Pigs entertain friends with a good round
    of crud.

Pig isn't dainty, Pig isn't a prude.

In fact, when he's hungry,

Pig's often quite rude!

continued

It's easy to call Pig a porker and sneer,

But Pig's got some traits we all could revere.

Pig is straightforward; Pig knows his mind.

To get to their goal, Pigs don't mind getting
  slimed.

Pig picks his battles but loses the bulge,

And he's got other tips he can divulge.

How to be lazy when crazy won't do.

How to look tranquil when dining for two.

Pig, teach me courage to fight the good fight!

And please bless me, Pig, with a sound
  appetite!

PRAYER FOR
SELF-WORTH

This is a prayer to Tiny Finch,

Who proves the power of an inch.

The Finch is small except in song.

It proves appearances can be wrong.

Golden-feathered, golden-tongued,

The Finch is known by what is sung.

God of Tiny Fairy Finch,

Teach me not to ever flinch.

Teach me, Bird, by your example

That all of us are more than ample.

PRAYER FOR OPTIMISM

This is a prayer to the Lord of Rabbit,
The Creature who makes having high hopes
    a habit.
Bunnies are bouncy. Bunnies have springs.
Their back legs love pouncing and leaping
    in rings.
Bunnies have ears just as long as their legs.
Their hearing keeps steering them all while
    they play.
Bunnies have cottontails, white balls of fluff,
That flash like full moons when they jump
    high enough.
Bunnies are munchers. They nibble on greens.
They let us eat lettuce by sharing like queens.

Our carrots are borrowed from Bunnies'

    supply.

That's why they have such a sparkling eye.

Bunnies keep gardens from growing too big.

Although they are small, Bunnies eat just

    like Pig.

Bunnies are shy and they run at the sight

Of dogs which can give them a terrible fright.

Yet Bunnies are daring. They leap into view

Whenever the garden has something

    brand new.

The message of Bunny by now must be clear:

If you don't like it there, hop right over here!

PRAYER FOR GENTLENESS

This is a prayer to the God of Whales,

Gigantic creatures with butterflies' tails.

Whales cross the ocean singing their songs,

Telling each other just where they have gone.

Whales live on plankton, tiny and green.

Although they look fierce, they're not what

    they seem.

Whales are not fishes, it now must be said.

They breathe just like us through a hole in

    their head.

Whales make good friends. They travel

    in pods—

Best friends and buddies with incredible bods.

Whales know the mysteries found in the deep.

They share them by singing while the rest
   of us sleep.
The lesson of Whale, you must realize,
Is to always be gentle—whatever your size.

PRAYER TO TRUST PROVIDENCE

This is a prayer to the God of Wrens,

To the God of Ducks and the God of Hens,

To the God of Swans gently gliding,

To the God of Sparrows loud, colliding,

God of all these feathered ones,

Teach me how to trust what comes.

Teach me live as fowl do,

Knowing God will see me through.

Like the birds alert to seeds,

Let me see you meet my needs.

Teach me trust as seasons flow

These will be enough, and so,

Let me sing with open heart,

"God is bountiful," that's the start.

Let my song rise in the wind.

The gentle universe is my friend.

Like the birds with their sweet nest,

Let me build from good the best.

God of Winged Creatures, be

My lesson in hospitality.

Teach me "take" as well as "give."

Teach me "joy" as well as "live."

God of Winged Singers Free,

Help me sing the song of me.

PRAYER FOR JOYFUL EXPANSION

This prayer goes out to Sweet Gazelle,

Whose burgeoning joy says, "Life is swell!"

Your leaping heart so filled with glee—

Like your cousin Okapi.

You know no hurdle too big to handle.

You jump the flame of any candle.

Burning bright like leaping fire,

Your lesson is, "We can go higher!"

PRAYER FOR
SELF-CONTAINMENT

This is a prayer to the God of Wolf,

Whose lesson is, "Respect yourself."

On wintry nights when blizzards snarl,

The Wolf Tribe raises a silvery howl.

Traveling by moonlight, a shadow in trees,

The Wolves range as freely as they please.

Mated for life to a spouse most loyal,

The Wolf has a loyalty quite royal.

Running in packs, a brigade of friends,

Wolves take to earth as each year ends.

Snuggled in warm, deep in Mother Earth,

Wolves rear their cubs to know the worth

Of self-containment far from men

Who do not view Wolf as their friend.

continued

Alone, aloof, misunderstood,

Wolf finds comfort in brotherhood.

Often hunted, seldom caught,

The Wolf says, "Value what you've got."

In forest glen most comfortable,

The Wolf says, "Learn you're valuable."

PRAYER FOR INTUITION

God of Gentle Brown-eyed Doe,

Help me know the things I know.

Let me know the gentle grace

To sense the world and know my place.

Give me guidance to perceive

The things I want, the things I need.

Help me make my peaceful way.

Give me safety while I play

God of Gentle Brown-eyed Doe,

Help me, like you, pure goodness show.

PRAYER FOR
SELF-KNOWLEDGE

This prayer goes to Ape and Monkey.

You cheer me up when I feel funky.

The Great Baboon, the Chimpanzee—

Your monkey business looks like me.

You're the mirror of almost here,

The parts of me I sometimes fear.

Gorilla and Orangutan,

Your swinging teaches, "Yes, I can!"

Your diet of berries and bananas can

Make me pause in my shenanigans.

Monkeys do what monkeys see.

Your lesson is "Think first" to me.

PRAYER FOR INNOCENCE

🐾

This is a prayer to the Lord of Sheep,

The ones who count us off to sleep.

Oh God of Lambs, Oh Shepherd Dear,

Please help us keep you safely near.

From Lamb I learn such gentle ways

As Jesus taught in olden days.

Lamb roams freely, needs no fence.

His nature tends to be innocence.

Lamb will follow where he's led.

So lead me carefully, keep me fed.

Our modern world is not the place

For Lambs' and Shepherds' gentle pace.

Lord of the Lamb, so soft and wooly,

Help me be sweet and never to bully.

continued

Lord of the Lamb who guides his sheep.

Softly count me off to sleep.

PRAYER FOR SHREWDNESS

God of Coyote, God of Fox,

Teach me with your wily walks.

Make me clever, make me shrewd.

Help me spot my greater good.

Independence marks your tracks.

Give me sense to face the facts.

Teach me run when danger's near.

Teach me listen to my fear.

Teach me know my friend and foe.

Teach me stay and teach me go.

Let me learn your cunning ways

And bring protection to my days.

PRAYER FOR
FAITH IN MYSTERY

God of Raven, God of Crow,

God of Darkness, gently show

The peace that comes from trusting night

To be the brother of the light.

Just as sunlight brings us shadow,

Darkness teaches us to value

Eyes of insight shining bright,

Clarity born of inner sight.

God of Raven, God of Crow,

Mystery cloaks your presence so

Seeing you we fill with awe.

You teach us by your beak and claw.

Winged in jet obsidian,

You teach us mystery is our friend.

God of Raven, God of Crow,

We learn by what you will not show.

Robed in darkness, cloaked in black,

Seeing you, we circle back.

"Seek the light, but honor night."

Raven, Crow, you set things right.

Guide to wisdom's other shore,

You remind us we are more.

PRAYER FOR
GRACEFUL GROWTH

This is a prayer to Brother Snake.

Please teach me to imitate

Your gentle way like water flowing,

The way you try without it showing.

Teach me, Snake, your self-containment.

Help me shed my earthly raiment

Whenever life has turned it dull.

Teach me, Snake, that changing will

Bring a brighter hue to bear.

Brother Snake, help me to dare

Strike with passion, be an arrow,

An energy that's true and narrow.

Snake, the fine line that you draw

Fills the heart with temperate awe.

Silent being, silent flowing,

Teach me, Snake, we learn by going.

PRAYER TO SEE PAST APPEARANCES

The animal I like the best

Is the one you'd never guess.

I'm talking Hippopotamus—

The hippest beast of all of us.

Hippo wears a suit of gray.

It suits the mud where Hippos play.

Prone to wallow where none follow,

Hippo is a daring fellow.

Hippo haunts the river's bank—

A gap-toothed, grinning, swimming tank.

Now you see him, now you don't—

Hippo sinks and then he floats.

Timid for so large a fellow,

Hippo's got a shape like jello.

He can roar if you intrude,

But Hippo hates to be so rude.

Hippo knows he's big and scary,

But he'd rather be quite merry.

See his giant, gap-tooth grin?

That's the face of my best friend.

I get dirty; he gets muddy.

It's nice to have a big-bod buddy.

God of Hippopotamus,

Give my friend a hug and kiss.

Tell him he's my favorite sub—

The U-boat I have learned to love.

PRAYER FOR CAUTION

This is a prayer to the God of Crocs.

Where I've got teeth, they've got flocks.

When I want a toothy smile,

I look to find a Crocodile.

I check the swamp—

They like the damp.

I'm a very cautious wader

Since sooner or later I spot a 'Gator.

That's Croc's first cousin, Alligator.

As a friend you have to hate her.

She smiles and blinks her beady eyes.

Then she gets you by surprise.

She's not friendly.

She's just hungry.

God forbid, you get her angry.

Crocs and 'Gators both can swim

Or slither up the bank, my friend.

Watch out for sleeping, gray-barked logs.

Crocs and 'Gators are not dogs.

They do not bark to warn their prey.

Help me, God, to stay away!

PRAYER FOR RESILIENCE

This is a prayer for Kangaroo,

The one who travels one for two.

Roo carries its youngster in its pouch—

Fine when no one is a grouch.

Kangaroo is no such thing.

Roo leaps on legs that like to spring.

Hopping like a giant bunny,

Kangaroo can look quite funny—

But he's followed by a tail

Much more mighty than it's frail.

When he lashes that tail out,

You might want to walk about.

Kangaroo is more than Aussie.

Kangaroo is pretty bossy.

Yes, he is mighty cute,

But Kangaroo packs quite a boot.

Leaping up when he goes down,

Kangaroo is like a clown

Who makes us laugh at all his folly,

Teaching smile when times aren't jolly.

Just bounce back says his behavior—

Optimism is a savior.

God of leaping Kangaroo,

Teach me how to bounce back, too.

PRAYER FOR PERSISTENCE

This is a prayer to the God of Camel,

That humpbacked, swaying, braying mammal.

The desert's ship through arid lands,

The Camel sails across the sands.

Trackless wastes pass underfoot

While Camel finds the surest route

From one oasis to another,

All without a drink of water.

Camel teaches me persistence,

Persevere in every instance.

Camel teaches prudence, too.

He knows it's best not to eschew

Any chance to quench your thirst

Cause things could go from bad to worse.

PRAYER FOR SOLITUDE

This is a prayer to the God of Skunk
Who may have wanted to be a monk
And live alone without annoyance
Hence the "scents" of his avoidance.
Cloaked in black and cowled in white,
The Skunk looks like some acolyte.
Black and white just like the paper,
Skunk exudes a potent rapier.
"En garde" is what Skunk's scent declares.
Why can't you leave me to my prayers?

PRAYER FOR COURAGE

This is a prayer to the God of Spider.

That acrobat, that graceful glider

Spinning webs of gossamer

And filling hearts with awesome fear.

Spider's web is a tracery

That says there's more to make of me.

One itsy rope at a time,

Like Tarzan on a tiny vine,

Spider swoops from heights to depths

And teaches dare without regrets.

Help me go beyond my fear,

To leap and let the net appear.

PRAYER FOR GRACE IN AMBIGUITY

This is a prayer to the God of Hen,

Of all God's creatures the most Zen.

Did Chicken come before the egg?

Or vice versa, you might beg?

Why did Chicken cross the road?

Or is that just for Hen to know?

Help me, Hen, hatch my ideas

Like your eggs in twos and threes.

Teach me, Hen, to bide my time

And lay my plans 'til they are fine.

Remember, Hen, that next to Rooster,

I remain your biggest booster.

PRAYER FOR STUBBORN INDIVIDUALISM

This is a prayer to Zippy Zebra

Whose bold stripes say, "So glad to

see ya."

Zebra is crisply black and white,

A headline that can kick and bite.

Just as cranky as a mule,

The Zebra is nobody's fool.

Not a pet or beast of burden,

The Zebra likes to get his word in.

He'll argue if you try to train him.

He'll fight instead of let you

tame him.

Just as wild as he appears,

A Zebra can go for years,

Lurking through the veldt's tall grasses

Stubborn as a horse's ass is.

PRAYER FOR FORTITUDE

This is a prayer to the God of Bison,

The Buffalo who makes us think twice and

Learn from our errors and own our mistakes

He asks us have the courage it takes

To hold, to love, to see the Earth

As a gentle garden that is worth

Humans conscious of their place

As guardians of a sacred space.

Where all are brothers, all are tribe.

Buffalo helps us go inside.

"Always know the things you know,"

So teaches Sacred Buffalo.

PRAYER TO ACCEPT LIFE'S SEASONS

God of Aspen, God of Meadow,

God of Sunlight, God of Shadow,

God of Autumn, God of Spring,

God of All the Seasons bring

Wisdom to my changing heart,

Grace to know my changing part.

God who partners snow and summer,

God who paints both green and umber,

Make me open to the shifts

Of summer sun and winter drifts.

Help me love your dappled good

And see the shades of brotherhood.

PRAYER TO LOVE DIFFERENCES

God of Valley, God of Mountain,

God of River, God of Fountain,

God of Country, God of Town,

God of Air and God of Ground,

God of Large and God of Small,

Show me God in one and all.

No one's different; no one's wrong.

All are valued; all belong.

God of Ocean, flow that's tidal,

Help me see this earth as tribal.

God of Shore of Silken Sand,

Like you, let me be promised land.

Grant me safety; grant me grace

To give my brethren each a place.

God of Marble, God of Granite,

Help me love this garden planet!

PRAYER FOR PROTECTION AND GUIDANCE

🌿

God of Sage and God of Cedar,

God of Brook and God of Beaver,

Make my home a sacred space.

Give my heart a safer place

To seek your wisdom and your will,

To see your view as from a hill,

A higher ground that lends perspective.

Higher Forces, be protective.

God of Cedar, God of Sage,

Ancient Powers, share your age.

Help me act with elder's wisdom

To protect your earthly kingdom.

Give my heart the gift of learning

Like your kind, to be discerning.

Help me pause before I act.

Help me keep my feet on track.

God of Sage and God of Cedar,

Let me follow, you be leader.

PRAYER FOR HUMILITY IN CHANGE

God of Clouds, God of Vapor,

God of Mists, Mysterious Nature,

Teach me by your changing face

To know my value and my place.

All is passing, all is changing.

Guide me, God, in rearranging

Every spark and part of me

To better live my destiny.

May I walk in humble ways,

Like the wind-blown clouds in days

Of gentle blue and snowy white.

Guide me, God, to do things right.

PRAYER IN
TIME OF LOSS

God of Winter, God of Frost,

Teach me how to weather loss

God of Cold and Seasons Chill,

Teach me that my losses will

Turn to value, turn to gold,

Just as spring turns warm from cold.

God of All Forbidding Things,

Teach me that this hardship brings

Lessons, blessings, gifts, and more—

Like sea shells left upon the shore.

Every grief still turns to gain.

Please give me strength to weather pain.

God of Snowfall, God of Ice,

I turn to you for warm advice.

continued

As my heart feels close to frozen,

Show the lesson you have chosen.

God of Snowflake, God of Winter,

Unlock my door and quickly enter.

In my snowy winter heart,

Build a glowing gentle hearth.

God of Winter, God of Frost,

In you I find what I have lost.

PRAYER TO
SERVE UNITY

God of Rock and God of Stone,

God of Antler, God of Bone,

God of Sea Shell, God of Water,

God of Salmon and of Otter,

God of every living thing,

Help my heart to always bring

Gentle love and true devotion

To your land and to your ocean.

Show me how to love your forests,

Love your birds, their gentle chorus.

Teach me how to walk this earth

With all the honor that it's worth.

Teach me, God, to love creation.

We are one, a global nation.

A B O U T   T H E   A U T H O R

Julia Cameron, best-selling author of *The Artist's Way*, *The Vein of Gold*, *The Right To Write*, *Blessings*, *Heart Steps*, and *The Dark Room*, is an active artist who teaches internationally. A poet, playwright, novelist, essayist, and award-winning journalist, she has extensive credits in film, television, and theater. Cameron's poetry album, *This Earth* (music by Tim Wheater), won *Publishers Weekly*'s Best Original Score award.